Doorkeeper of the Heart

Doorkeeper

CHARLES UPTON

of the Heart

Versions of Rabi'a

NEW YORK · PIR PRESS · 2003

Published by
Pir Press (imprint of Pir Publications, Inc.)
227 West Broadway
New York, New York 10013

ISBN 1-879708-20-5

Printed in the United States of America

Cover Painting: Maria Zerres

May God steal from you
All that steals you from Him.

RABI'A

Introduction

Rabi'a's History

Rabi'a al-'Adawiyya, a major saint of Islam and one of the central figures in Sufi tradition, was born (according to one reckoning) in 717 A.D., and died in 801. She was born and lived in Basra in what is now Iraq, the ancient Mesopotamia. Stories about her and poems attributed to her—which make up the substance of this book—have come down to us through many Sufi writers, including Attar, her major biographer, and al-Ghazzali—the central pole where Sufi lore and orthodox Islam meet.

Little is known of her actual life, and that little is a mixture of factual information and hagiography—saint stories—another kind of "fact".

The "real" facts are brief: she was born into a poor family. During a famine both her parents died, and she and her sisters were separated. Homeless and vulnerable, she was captured and sold as a slave. Later on she was freed by her master, and may have made her living as a fluteplayer at one time. She may have made the pilgrimage to Mecca. In later life she became famous as a saint; she was offered money, houses, and proposals of marriage, but preferred to remain single, and live in humble surroundings—some texts say in a "ruin"—where she spent her time praying, keeping house, performing spiritual excercises, and receiving visitors; the stories of her interactions with those who came to challenge or learn from her make up the bulk of the Rabi'a material as we know it.

Rabi'a's Friends

Many of the anecdotes about Rabi'a, including poems attributed to
her, are in the form of dialogues between her and her friends, simi-
lar in many ways to the teaching dialogues between Muhammed and
his Companions, Jesus and his Apostles, Buddha and his Disciples,
Socrates and his Banqueters. Chief among these friends were Sufyan
al-Thawri, her closest male companion, Rabah al-Qays, a well-known
ascetic of the same school as Sufyan; and Mariam of Basra, her most
devoted female disciple, who became her servant. Another name fre-
quently associated with hers is Hasan of Basra, well-known leader of
an extreme school of world-denying ascetics—but scholarship seems
to show that he was around eleven years old when Rabi'a died, so
many of the stories of their encounters may actually represent a con-
troversy between their schools. Hasan, in these stories, is often the
butt of Rabi'a's sharper wit, deeper wisdom, and greater spiritual
power; the intent may be to pose Rabi'a, the fully developed mystic,
against Hasan, the narrow-minded ascetic, to whose surface knowl-
edge she (formed by the same tradition) held the inner spiritual key.
There is also a story that she once visited and was eagerly acknowl-
edged by the great Egyptian Sufi Du'l-Nun, "King of the Fish" (who
may or may not have had a cultic relationship with the Authurian
"Fisher King" figure)* —but this may indicate (I suspect) more a
common inner tradition than a personal encounter.

Biographical Legends

Most of the stories about Rabi'a are "legendary"—meaning that
they don't correspond to the Western sense of factual history
because they seem more symbolic than factual in intent—as if the
actual events of people's lives can't be just as "symbolic" as any
invented romance. So here are seven legends of Rabi'a—which, if
"character is fate" are true as any date carved in stone:

*The stories of Du'l-Nun's meetings with symbolic maidens in the wilderness
and on the shore of the sea carry to me a definite Arthurian flavor.

(1)

On the night Rabi'a was born, there was no cloth to wrap her in, and no oil for the lamps. Her mother asked her father to borrow oil from a neighbor, but he refused because he was under a vow never to ask for anything from anyone but God.

Then he fell asleep, and the Prophet Muhammed appeared to him in a dream: "Don't worry," he said, "the daughter just born to you will be a great saint; 70,000 of my followers will venerate her. Tomorrow you are to write a letter to the Amir, reminding him that he is in the habit of praying to me a hundred prayers every night, and four hundred on Friday. Say that since he missed last Friday, he has to make up for it by giving you four hundred *dinars*."

Rabi'a's father wrote and sent the letter—and when the Amir received it he gave his command: "Give two thousand *dinars* to the sage who has written this, telling him that I would willingly grant him an audience, except that it would be an insult to him: I'll travel to his house instead, and rub my beard on his threshold."

And the father named his daughter "Rabi'a," which means "the fourth."

(2)

After death and poverty had scattered Rabi'a's family, she was approached by a slave-trader; she tried to run, but slipped and sprained her wrist. When she knew freedom was lost, she cried: "O God! I am an orphan, and am about to be a slave—on top of that, my wrist is broken. But that's not what I care about; the thing I have to know is: are you satisfied with me?"

Immediately a Voice answered her: "Don't worry—on the Day of Resurrection your rank will be so high that even the closest companions of God will envy you."

Then Rabi'a submitted to the Will of god, and became a slave.

(3)

In her life as a slave, Rabi'a found time for her worship of God by doing without sleep. She fasted and prayed. One night her master awoke, looked down from the window of his house into the court-yard, and saw Rabi'a in prayer. As he was watching her he was amazed to see a lamp appear above her head, suspended in mid-air; the light from this miraculous lamp lit up the whole house. Terrified and astonished, he went back to bed, and sat wondering until dawn. Then he called Rabi'a to him, confessed what he had seen, and gave her her freedom, with the option of staying on with him if she want-ed to. She asked permission to leave and it was granted; so she went out of the house, and out of that city, and into the desert to pray.

* * *

A number of stories about Rabi'a have to do with her pilgrimage to Mecca to see the Kaaba. She never quite seemed to be able to get there—ultimately the Kaaba had to come to her instead (which seems to be a sort of reversal of the Muhammed-and-the-mountain story). Her difficulties in completing the pilgrimage seem to sym-bolize both the struggles of the mystic path, and her own difficul-ty in coming to terms with the conventional Islamic community; and the Kaaba's coming to her may also point to the truth that the last (as well as the first) step on that path is taken not by the mys-tic, but by God Himself.

(4)

On pilgrimage to Mecca, Rabi'a went into the desert leading an ass to carry her baggage; but the ass died. Others in the caravan offered to help her but she refused; instead she prayed to God, "Is *this* how a great King treats a weak, helpless woman he has invited to visit his House?" Immediately the ass came back to life, stood up, and Rabi'a continued on her journey.

(5)

It took Ibrahim Ibn Adham fourteen years to reach the Kaaba in pilgrimage, because he said long prayers at every shrine along the way—but when he got there, there was no Kaaba to be seen. "What is this?" he asked himself. "Have I gone blind?"

"No," a Voice said, "you can't see the Kaaba because it has gone out to meet a woman." Burning with jealousy, Ibrahim ran toward the outskirts of Mecca till he ran into Rabi'a, who was just arriving. He turned around, and saw the Kaaba back in its usual place. Then he turned to Rabi'a.

"What's this craziness you've brought into the world, woman?" he demanded.

"It's not I who am the author of craziness," she replied, "but you. You were crazy enough to take fourteen years to get to the Kaaba with your ritual prayer, while I, with my inner prayer, am here already.

(6)

Once upon a time several different men wanted to marry Rabi'a, including Abd al-Wahid Ibn Zayd, Hasan of Basra, the Amir of Basra himself, and even the provincial governor. This was her answer to the Amir:

"I'm not interested, really, in 'possessing all you own,'
Nor in 'making you my slave,'
Nor in having my attention distracted from
God even for a split second."

And she told the governor:

"Control *yourself*: Don't let others control you.
Instead, better share your inheritance with them,
And suffer like they do the common suffering of the time.
As for you: Remember the day of your death.
As for me: Whatever bride-price you come up with,

Understand that the Lord *I* worship can double it.

"So good-bye."

* * *

Several of Rabi'a's poems have to do with her habit of keeping all-night vigils. In line with Islamic tradition, she practiced the ancient technique of combating spiritual sleep by avoiding physical sleep—of sitting up on the roof all night, while the lights are out and the consensus of the day is asleep, watching the Universe turn. There's even a story that, after an accusing dream, Rabi'a never slept again as long as she lived. (Knowing the feats of the Hindu and Tibetan yogis I can't call this impossible—but I suspect that what this story refers to is an unbroken stream of consciousness through the waking state, the dream state, and deep sleep—which may, in fact, come to the same thing.)

(7)

Once upon a time Rabi'a fasted, prayed and stayed awake for seven days and nights. Then somebody brought her a bowl of food. Rabi'a accepted it, and went to find a lamp—but when she came back with the lamp she saw that a cat had knocked over the bowl. "So I'll drink water instead," she said to herself, and went to find the water-jug—but by the time she came back with it, the lamp had gone out. "Then I'll drink my water in the dark," she said—but then, without warning, the jug fell out of her hands, and broke into a thousand pieces. At that point she cried out, loud, loud, loud, almost loud enough to set the whole house on fire. "God! God!" she cried, "What are You trying to do to me?"

"Be careful," a Voice answered. "If you really want me to, I'll fill your heart with all the pleasures of This World, and empty it of all your care for Me. *You* want something and *I* want something, and these desires cannot be mixed."

After this, Rabi'a gave up all worldly hope.

vi

Jelaluddin Rumi is widely recognized as the greatest Sufi poet, if not the greatest spiritual writer, of all time; and so it is illuminating to compare Rabi'a with Rumi, to get some sense of where she stands.

First, she stands some five hundred years earlier—close to the beginnings of Sufi poetry as we know it. If Rumi is the Ocean, Rabi'a is the Well. It is clearly true that, for sheer ecstatic energy, for multidimensional meaning, and for compacted lore Rumi is richer by far. Rabi'a, on the other hand, has the virtues of maidenly simplicity, and the virgin blade; along with the taste of wine, she carries also the taste of water—a far more precious substance when you live, like Rabi'a did, in the desert of God.

Rumi is expansive, his richness of imagery is nearly unparalleled; he has the power of reading the world like a book, of seeing a reflection of the Divine Face in every visible form; and those of us who have not despaired of life on Earth prize this quality today, living as we do in an age when the Greco-Christian denial of Earthly reality has so terribly come home to roost. Rabi'a, by comparison, is sometimes faulted for her narrower piety and asceticism; Madam El Sakkakini, for one, in her book on Rabi'a (cf. Bibliography), seems almost scandalized by it, and goes far to prove that Rabi'a finally transcended her pious fear and addiction to asceticism, and became a "true Sufi," i.e., a person who had come to terms with his or her community, and so has the maturity and stability to confront spiritual experience without becoming, to use Gurdjieff's term, a "lunatic".

In all places and times, this is the Ideal—but there are more ways than one of coming to terms with society, with community, with consensus—and one of these is the way of the Hermit, aloof yet available, pointing to more than community knows. Rabi'a's asceticism has this quality; and when asceticism proves to have a deep spiritual and cultural influence, like hers did, there is usually a good reason for it. For the early Christians, the need was to separate themselves, spiritually if not physically, from a powerful, massive, oppressive, degenerate, and dying Roman Empire—to preserve the spark of revelation and grace for centuries inside an alien world that denied it in every particular. The Islamic experience, on the other hand, was radically different: by the time Islam broke free from its desert home, Rome was dead, and the entire ancient world from Spain to India was a vacuum begging to be filled. The stunning ease with which Islam conquered over half the known world bred an easy identification between spiritual potency and worldly success, and a parallel misunderstanding and distrust of monasticism: what could it possibly be for, they asked, if not to shelter some kind of anti-social self-indulgence? The Sufis, of course, kept a social form similar to monasticism inside the greater Islamic consensus (though they had to go underground from time to time to do it)—but orthodox Islam officially frowned upon permanent separation from society as a path to God, a little like our own Reformation Protestants; both were expansive, masculine trading societies which throve on the active life.

Rabi'a's experience, on the other hand, was not unlike that of the early Christians. She was a member of the older population of Mesopotamia, recently conquered and converted to Islam by the Arab invaders who now made up the ruling class. She was of the poorest class of her society, a slave at one time, later a freed slave, undoubtedly living an even more precarious life for a while, as freed slaves often do. Apparently she was not under the guardianship of any male relative, the most common form of social and economic protection for an unmarried women, so it's likely she paid for her freedom with her security. Rumi, on the other hand, although he had to flee his native city of Balkh in Afghanistan (either because his father quarreled with the Sultan, or because of the threatening invasion by Tamerlane), was able to move into a comfortable professorship in Konya of Rum (in what is now Turkey), and found an order, the Mevlevis, which was patronized by the Turkish Sultans during much of its history. But by the time Rabi'a's fame as a holy woman had spread, and she was being offered money, houses, and proposals of marriage, her early hardships had already formed her character: to accept a gift from This World was to turn her back on the God who had sustained her when This World had nothing to offer but a whip. We may unfurl splendid and legitimate ideals of the Complete Man as one who has both this world and the next in his pocket—but God may have other plans, and unless we want to limit Providence to the realm of obvious psychological and social good, we will have to preserve living examples of the Poor in Spirit, who have struggled, seen, and been touched by God in the ruins of this world.

Rabi'a's "Christianity"

Possibly because her character was formed in suffering and exploitation, some have speculated that Rabi'a was the product of a Christian influence at work in Islam. Of course Islam was never preserved from Christian influence; the Qur'an represents Jesus as a prophet second only to Muhammad in importance. But is there any justification for saying that Rabi'a, or the Sufis themselves, are "Christian" in some hidden way?

St. Augustine said somewhere that Christianity, as a primordial religion, has always existed; although Christ is the center of it, it did not begin (in terms of time) with the life of Jesus. Idries Shah (and Gurdjieff, if the truth be known) made the same claim for Sufism; it is primordial, as old as the human race; the first Sufi was Adam.

We can understand these claims in at least two different ways. In one, the Prophet or Redeemer has no end or beginning because he is an eternal emanation of God, a Spirit of Guidance who is available to the Human form under any and all circumstances because he is the seed or prototype of that Form. In the other, there is seen to exist in the culture-sphere of the Near and Middle East an immensely old tradition of human progress, a tradition which gave us the first grain, the first writing, the first cities, the first bronze, the first iron—a tradition which understands all these steps in social and technical development in terms of a Cosmic perspective, which sees the material and spiritual growth of Humanity as crucial to the destiny of the Earth, and that destiny as occupying one stage in the evolution of the Universe, in its long journey back to the Source which gave it birth.

Mystics tend to be overt or covert universalists. Seeing the one root of all, they can see the "transparent unity of religions" without thereby falling into a shallow eclecticism. In both Islam and

Christianity they have had such wide perspectives of truth forced upon them that they often found it difficult to speak without being accused of heresy. Thus the Sufis, who drew on traditions older than Muhammed (as Muhammed himself did: he was in fact a missionary of the Hanifs or "penitents," a syncretistic school of Jewish-Christian-Essene mystics), and who understood these traditions in a deeper sense than the religious literalists, sometimes had a hard row to hoe. And Rabiʻa was no exception. She was not physically martyred, like al-Hallaj, but she was in some sense socially martyred, because her relationship with God did not allow her to obey certain social (if not legal) imperatives: to marry, to have children, to get ahead in the world for the greater good of the Islamic community. Although she did not make a point of rebelliously violating the social norms of her time, she was profoundly outside them; and how disturbing it must have been to the fathers of that community to be faced with a living exemplar of the spiritual life who would accept neither the material nor the "spiritual" rewards that community had to offer. Her refusal called into question the whole Islamic (and Semitic) tendency to identify community consensus with the Will of God—and yet they could not reject her; her piety, her renunciation, her gnosis, could not be veiled.

The relationship, in Islam, between "this world" and "the next" is very close to that in Christianity—and yet the two are so far apart that they can be called, to use Blake's terminology, true "contraries". Christianity has tended to see this world as real—and really fallen. It follows from this that monastic withdrawal from the world is the straight path of holiness, and that those who deal with the world (even if they are ecclesiastics) are almost justified in acting profanely, since they are dealing with a profane reality. In Islam, on the other hand, the world is seen less as a fallen reality, and more as a veil, or seventy veils, over the Divine Face. (Gothic Christianity actually tended to have a similar view, in which it may have been influenced by contacts with the Muslim world.) Consequently it was easier, at least in theory, for the Muslim to be "in the world but not of it," and to make sacred, as far as this is possible, the work of the world: commerce, craftsmanship, sexuality, and war.

The Prophet declared that there was to be "no monasticism in Islam"; but by "monasticism" he did not mean "contemplation".

Even in his lifetime certain of his companions were "companions of the bench," who kept apart from the work of the world, spent their time in the mosque in spiritual exercises and contemplation, and were honored. In other words, Islam rejects not "withdrawal from the community of all believers"—which implies that this community, as a whole, has one foot in the next world already.

But Rabi'a, at one point, and as far as she could, withdrew physically. Asceticism of a very "Christian" type (really a universal one) was practiced by the Sufis, as a part of their repertoire during most of their history, and this was particularly true of the school of Hasan of Basra, who spent his time bewailing and belittling This World in favor of the Next, somewhat in the spirit of John the Baptist. (One wonders whether the Essenes, with whom John appears to have been connected, and who are thought to be the ancestors of the present Mandaeans of Iraq, were not an influence here.)

Al-Ghazzali calls Rabi'a a prime exemplar of the Station of Love—which would place her, according to the Islamic view, in the same Station of the Way as Jesus, who is also seen as the founder of monastic asceticism. This seems accurate. But Rabi'a speaks to us just as clearly out of other Stations as well: the Station of Repentance, the Station of World-alienation (the Gnostic Crisis), and the Station of Fear—Fear of Divine Judgement as the necessary purification that comes before the unfoldment of Divine Gnosis. And, in the realm of asceticism, she seems to have done Hasan of Basra one better. While never quite free from her fear of the Judgment of God, she seems to have been among those who introduced into Sufism the view that the true worship of God entails sacrifice of the desire for both this world and the next (a view common to Hinduism and Buddhism, both of which distinguish between the paradise earned by merit, and final Liberation). There is also a tradition that Rabi'a was the one who introduced the image of wine into Islamic poetry, as a symbol of religious ecstacy—a stage development considering the strict Muslim prohibition of alcohol. Some would conjecture that this indicates a Christian influence (though I suspect it derives from earlier Persian poetry), but be that as it may, Rabi'a was devout Muslim, with no heterodox tendencies except those common to all mystics. There are always those who, failing to deeply enough grasp their own traditions, view their own esoteric lore as a pollution by foreign devils.

*   *   *

It wouldn't be strictly accurate to say that this is a book of the poems of Rabi'a. Apart from the fact that it also contains fables *about* her, the truth is that we don't know for sure whether she actually wrote poems, though a number of well-known poems are attributed to her. She may have composed poems; she may have transmitted certain traditional sacred poetry as a part of her teaching—poetry she may have learned during her career as a flute player, if it's true she was a sacred musician serving the Sufi community.* In any case, the poems and fables in this book are based on sayings attributed to her, or stories about her, which have passed through a long line of Sufi historians, commentators and translators for almost thirteen hundred years, during which time anything that was not already a poem has gotten so close to poetry, through the refinement of re-telling, that I was inspired to take the final step.

In producing these versions of Rabi'a, I have in most cases been faithful to the literal meaning of my English sources. When I departed from the literal, I did so in four ways: by extending a statement into metaphor; by adding (in a few cases) a new image or statement to bridge a weak place in the original; by radically compressing a loose prose paragraph into verse; and (in a very few cases) by following a spark struck off the flint of the original, when I thought I saw beneath the skin of the text, and wrote what I saw.

---

*The first line of Rumi's *Mathnavi* is: "Listen to the sound of the reed!" The original word is "ney," which also means "flute." Compare the words of Jesus, talking about John the Baptist: "Who did you go out into the desert to see? A reed shaken by the wind?"

Versions of Rabi'a

I am fully qualified to work as a doorkeeper, and for this reason:
What is inside me, I don't let out:
What is outside me, I don't let in.
If someone comes in, he goes right out again—
He has nothing to do with me at all.
I am a Doorkeeper of the Heart, not a lump of wet clay.

Serving-girl:

"It's Spring, Rabi'a—
Why not come outside,
And look at all the beauty God has made!"

Rabi'a:

"Why not come inside instead, serving girl
And see the One who made it all—
Naked, without veil."

Cup, Wine, and Friend make three:
And I, thirsty with love, am Four...
The Cupbearer hands to each, one after another
The cup of unending joy:
If I look, it's Him I am looking for;
And if I arrive, then He is my eyes.

Don't blame me if I am in love with His beauty,
Because, by God, my ears cannot hear your slander.
Again and again, passion and the bitterness of attachment
Have turned my eyes into rivers.

My tears don't stop falling;
Nor am I allowed to stay with Him;
Nor can my burning eyes ever let me sleep.

I set up house for You in my heart
As a Friend that I could talk with.

Gave my body to someone else
Who wanted to embrace it.

This body, all in all, is good enough for embracing—

But the Friend who lives in my house
Is the lover of my Heart.

Where did you come from?
    From *There*.

Where are you going to?
    To *There*!

What are you doing here?
    I am *grieving*.

How so?
    I am eating *This* bread
    While doing *That* work!

I have two ways of loving You:
A selfish one
And another way that is worthy of You.
In my selfish love, I remember You and You alone.
In that other love, You lift the veil
And let me feast my eyes on Your Living Face.
That I remember You always, or that I see You face-to-face—
No credit to me in either:
The credit is to You in both.

If you hadn't singled me out to suffer your love,
I never would've brought you
All these lovers—
(Lord! Remember!)

If all the tortures of all the circles of Hell
Were put into one needle;

And if my right eye were lined with many such needles, all stuck
    in a row;

If my left eye twitched only once, and disturbed my prayer—
I would tear it out of its socket.

My peace, brothers, is in my aloneness
Because my Beloved is alone with me there—always.
I've found nothing to equal His love,
That love which harrows the sands of my desert.
If I die of desire, and He is still unsatisfied—
That sorrow has no end.

To abandon all He has made
To hold in my hand
Proof that He loves me—
This is the name of my quest.

O God, You know that the only thing I want in this life
Is to be obedient to Your command.
Even the living sight of my eyes
Is service at Your court.
I would never stop serving You, even for a single moment—
If it were up to me.
But You put me under the power of one of Your creatures—a man.

This is why I come to Your service late.

Marriage has to do with being—
But where can this being be found?
I should belong to you? What makes you think
I even belong to myself?
I am His—His!

God:

"So you call my Name—what are you asking for, really?
If it's Myself you want,
I'll open to you one spark of my Glory
And burn you out of existence."

Rabi'a:

"O Lord, I don't begin to have the power
To come that close to You—
So maybe You will give me
Just one grain of poverty instead?"

God:

"Poverty is the drought of My anger
Which I've placed on the human road.
When nothing is left between them and Me
But the width of a hair,
Then the hope of Union
Turns into the reality of Separation.
You are still hidden from Me
Under seventy veils—strip them off!
What can you say, or know, about Poverty
Until that Day?"

O God, take away the words of the devil
That mix with my prayer—

If not, then take my prayer as it is, devil and all.

O Children of Nothing!
Truth can't come in through your eyes,
Nor can speech go out through your mouth to find Him;
Hearing leads the speaker down the road to anxiety,
And if you follow your hands and feet you will arrive at confusion—
The real work is in the Heart:
Wake up your Heart! Because when the Heart is completely awake,
Then it needs no Friend.

The true Knower looks for a Heart that comes from God alone.
As soon as it is given to him, he gives it back again
So that God can hold it hidden in His Mystery,
Safe from the tampering of human hands.

Burn like wax, and give light.
Stitch like a needle, and look barren.
Last of all, become thin as a hair
So your work will not be wasted.

God doesn't make even those who curse Him destitute—
Then why shouldn't He provide for all the needs
Of someone whose soul is burning with love for Him?
Ever since I knew Him, I've turned my back on all He has made—
How then can I accept a gift of stolen goods?

One time I used the Sultan's lamp to patch a blouse—
But my heart closed up like a fist until I had undone every stitch.

I spun some yarn to sell for food
And sold it for two silver coins.
I put a coin in each hand
Because I was afraid
That if I put both together in one hand
This great pile of wealth might hold me back.

One day Rabi'a needed a piece of cloth,
So she gave a man three silver coins to buy one.

After he'd already started on his way, he turned back.
"My Lady," he said, "I forgot to ask:
    What color do you want?"

"So it's become a question of color, has it?" she replied.
"Give me back my money!"

And she threw it into the Tigris River.

Miracle Story

One day Hasan of Basra saw Rabi'a down by the riverside. He came up to her, spread his prayer-rug on the surface of the water, and said: "Come sit with me and pray."

"Do you really *have* to sell yourself in the market of this world to the consumers of the next?" said Rabi'a. Then she unrolled her own prayer-rug in thin air, and sat on it:

"What you did any fish can do, Hasan, and what I did any fly can do. Our real work is far beyond the work of fish and flies."

Miracle Story

One day Rabiʿa went into the mountains to pray, and all the animals, the deer and the wild asses, the goats and gazelles, came up to her, and gazed at her, and danced around her. Then, suddenly, Hasan of Basra showed up—and all the animals ran.

"Why did they make friends with you and run from me?" Hasan asked.

"What did you have for breakfast today?" asked Rabiʿa.

"Onions fried in lard."

"Why shouldn't they run from you," Rabiʿa answered, "since you eat their fat?"*

*Advice for teachers

Miracle Story

One day Rabiʻa and her serving-girl were getting ready to break a fast of several days. The serving-girl needed an onion and was about to go next door and borrow one, but Rabiʻa said: "Forty years ago I vowed never to ask for anything from anyone but God—we can do without onions."

Just then a bird flew over, and dropped an onion into Rabiʻa's frying pan, peeled and ready to fry.

"Interesting but not convincing," she said. "Am I supposed to believe that God is an onion-vender? I mean, really."

That day they fried their bread without onions.

Miracle Story

One year Rabi'a planted corn—but then a swarm of locusts arrived, and landed right on it.

Rabi'a prayed: "O God, this corn is my livelihood; it's taken both my money and my sweat. Who would You like me to give it to, then? To Your enemies or Your friends?"

As soon as she finished her prayer, the locusts rose in a cloud, and flew away, and were never seen again.*

*Advice for students

Miracle Story

One day, when Rabi'a was about to boil some meat, Hasan of Basra dropped by. "Speech about divine things is better food than anything cooked in a pan," she said, and laid the meat aside. They talked until evening.

Then they decided to break their fast. Rabi'a laid out dry bread and water, and then reached for the pan. She burnt her hand. The pan was bubbling over, the meat cooked. She took it out and served it: it was the best meat either of them had ever tasted.

"Good food for convalescents," Rabi'a said.

Miracle Story

One night when Rabi'a was asleep, a thief snuck into her room and stole her veil—but when he tried to get out again, he couldn't find the door. He dropped the veil, then found the door—but after he'd gone back to get the veil, he saw that the door had vanished. He dropped the veil again, saw the door—picked up the veil, the door was gone.

He went through this dance seven times. Then, from the corner of his room, a Voice spoke to him:

I wouldn't worry about it—she's been in Our keeping for many years, and not even the devil has had enough nerve to walk up and down in that country—how can a little pickpocket like you expect to walk up and down in her veil? If I were you, I'd forget it, because when one friend is asleep, the Other is awake."

Miracle Story

One day two holy men came to visit Rabi'a, hoping to get something to eat; they were sure that whatever food she gave them would be ritually pure since it was "obtained in a lawful manner."

After they had seated themselves, a cloth containing two loaves of bread was laid before them. Eagerly they reached for the food—

But before they could get it to their mouths, a hungry beggar appeared at the door. Rabi'a immediately gave him both loaves of bread.

This really bothered the two holy men, but they kept it to themselves.

Pretty soon a slave-girl arrived, carrying a load of freshly-baked bread. "My mistress sent this."

Rabi'a counted the loaves. "I don't think so," she said. "There are only eighteen here." Protests, denials—whatever the girl said, Rabia would not believe her.

(What happened was that the slave-girl had taken two loaves for herself.) So she went away and came back with the full twenty loaves. Rabi'a counted them again: "That's more like it."

So Rabi'a served the hungry holy men with twenty loaves instead of two. They were really baffled. "Two loaves, no loaves, twenty loaves—what does it all mean?" they asked.

"As soon as I saw you," said Rabi'a, "I could tell you were hungry. Two little loaves of bread—how could that be enough for two holy men? Then I remembered the Promise: 'You give one; I give ten.' So I gave two to the beggar—

"But when only eighteen came back, I knew that there was either something wrong with my prayer, or that somebody had sticky fingers."

Miracle Story

Rabi'a's niece Zulfa once asked her: "Aunt Rabi'a, why do you want to keep people from visiting you?"

"It's because I'm afraid they'll spread stories about me, saying I did things I never did, said things I never said."

But they say already that food appears miraculously in your house, and that you cook it without fire."

"Daughter of my brother, if such things ever showed up in this house, I wouldn't touch them with a ten-foot pole. Everything I have, I bought with my own money—*that's* why all things bless me."

The source of my grief and loneliness is deep in my breast.
This is a disease no doctor can cure.
Only Union with the Friend can cure it.
I was not born to the Grief of God—
I only grieve to be like those
Who are pierced with the Love of God—
I would be ashamed for my love
To appear less than the grief of others:
Therefore I grieve.

O God, You have promised to reward us for two things:
Pilgrimage, and the endurance of suffering—
But now You won't accept my Pilgrimage from me—
    how can I suffer this?
And what will You reward me with—O Just One—
for what I have suffered on the road?

No-one can claim to be sincere in love
Who doesn't forget the sting of the Master's whip
In the presence of the Master—

Just like those Egyptian women
Peeling fruit in the Pharaoh's kitchen
Who cut their hands to shreds when they saw
Beautiful Joseph stepping in the room,

And didn't even know it.

In love, nothing exists between breast and Breast.
Speech is born out of longing,
True description from the real taste.
The one who tastes, knows;
The one who explains, lies.
How can you describe the true form of Something
In whose presence you are blotted out?
And in whose being you still exist?
And who lives as a sign for your journey?

Love came out of the former Eternity,
Went away in to the Eternity to come,
And didn't see anyone in the eighteen-thousand worlds
Worthy to eat even one spoonful of its sweet sherbet—
And when Love reached Truth at last, only this word was left:
    He loves them;
    They also love Him.

Rabi'a:

"O God,
My heart is heavy, like lead, with anguish—
Where am I headed now?
I am only a handful of dust,
And your house is only a stone:
You are all I want in this world."

God:

"Watch out, Rabi'a—
You are getting near to the blood of the eighteen-thousand worlds.
If I were to show myself to the Universe as I am, the Universe
     would be shattered—
Do you want to destroy the Universe?
Don't you remember the story of Moses?
When he asked to see my Face
I scattered only a few atoms of revelation upon him,
And Sinai broke into forty pieces."

34

I saw Paradise at dawn, and desired it:
But then, out of His jealousy, God made me sick.*

*Can God be jealous?
Or is the jealousy really Rabi'a's,
Or mine? C.U.

One day Rabi'a was sick,
And so her holy friends came to visit her, sat by her bedside,
And began putting down the world.

"You must be pretty interested in this 'world,'" said Rabi'a,
"Otherwise you wouldn't talk about it so much:

Whoever breaks the merchandise
Has to have bought it first."

One day a rich merchant visited Rabi'a
And saw that she was living in a ruin:
So he gave her a thousand pieces of gold
And told her to buy a new house—

But the day she moved in, she became so fascinated
With the beautiful paintings that covered the walls
That she gave the rich man back his money
And went back to live in her ruin—why?

"Because I was mortally afraid
I might fall in love with that house," said Rabi'a.

Where a part of you goes
The rest of you will follow—given time.
You call yourself a teacher:
Therefore learn.

One day Hasan of Basra
Stuck his head out the window and cried
Till a drizzle of tears fell on Rabi'a
Passing in the street below.

"Those are proud tears, teacher," said Rabi'a
"Why not look into your heart and cry for real—
Cry till you've made a river so deep
That when you fish for your heart
You'll never find it there,
Until your hook is taken, at last
By the Lord of Power."

Sufiyan:

"This is my prayer: let God be satisfied with me."

Rabi'a:

"How dare you pray that—when *you* are not satisfied with God?"

"If I hate my sins, will God love me?"

"No—
But if He remembers you,
Then you will remember Him—

So stand in wait."

Blasphemy tastes like separation.
Faith brings joy, like a loving embrace.
This taste and this joy
Will be exposed tomorrow on the Day of Judgement.
Two groups will assemble on that plain—
One for Separation without Union:
One for Union without End.

Those for Separation will cry:

"Estrangement from Him
Makes a thousand days out of one second—
One night turns into a thousand years
Because of His suffering and His grief!"

And those for Union will sing:

"The hour of meeting
Opens the curtain of Union—
All separation from the Beloved
Now beats the parting drum."

If you're afraid that people might discover your sins,
Better start worrying they might find out about your good deeds!

I love God: I have no time left
In which to hate the devil.

O Lord,
You neither open to me the door of Your mansion
Nor let me rest in my own house—
Either invite me in at Mecca
Or leave me alone at Basra!

Once I wanted You so much
I didn't even dare walk past Your house—
And now
I am not even worthy to be let in.

I don't want the House,
I want the Lord of the House.
What could I do with the Kaaba if I had it?
It's the most famous idol in the world.
God isn't inside it, He isn't outside it—
The truth is, He doesn't need it.

"Rabi'a, Rabi'a—how do you see Paradise?"

"I see it like this:
'First the Neighbor, then the House.'"

O God,
If tomorrow on the Day of Judgement You send me to Hell
I will tell such a secret that Hell will break and run from me
Until it is a thousand years away.

Give the goods of this world to Your enemies—
Give the treasures of Paradise to Your friends—
But as for me—You are all I need.

O God!
If I adore You out of fear of Hell, burn me in Hell!
If I adore You out of desire for Paradise,
Lock me out of Paradise.
But if I adore You for Yourself alone,
Do not deny to me Your eternal beauty.

I carry a torch in one had
And a bucket of water in the other:
With these things I am going to set fire to Heaven
And put out the flames of Hell
So that voyagers to God can rip the veils
And see the real goal.

The call to prayer
Reminds me of the trumpet of the Day Judgement:
And whenever I see the snow falling
I see the white pages of my deeds,
Tossing in the wind.

If I beg You to forgive me, I lie.
If I ask myself to repent,
Someday I will have to repent
Of that repentance.

Your hope in my heart is the rarest treasure
Your Name on my tongue is the sweetest word
My choicest hours
Are the hours I spend with You—

O God, I can't live in this world
Without remembering You—
How can I endure the next world
Without seeing Your face?

I am a stranger in Your country
And lonely among Your worshippers:
This is the substance of my complaint.

My soul, how long will you go on falling asleep
And waking up again?
The time is almost here when you will fall into so deep a sleep
That only the Trumpet of Resurrection
Will have the power to wake you.

"I am the murderer of joy," said the Angel of Death,
"The widower of wives, the orphaner of children— "

"Why always run yourself down?" said Rabi'a—
"Why not say instead: 'I am he who brings friend and Friend
    together'?

"Why do you worship God, Rabi'a?"

"Why? Because there are seven degrees of 'why' which everyone
    must pass,
Seven steps on the ladder of Hell,
And everybody has to climb them,
In fear and terror,
Whether or not they want to,
Whether or not they can figure out
'Why'."

"Rabi'a—Rabi'a—how did you climb so high?"

"I did it by saying:

> 'Let me hide in You
> From everything that distracts me from You,
> From everything that comes in my way
> When I want to run to You.'"

"What miracles have you done, if any, Rabi'a?"

"If I were to admit to a miracle
I'd be worried it might bring in money—

So my answer is: not one!"

My Joy—
My Hunger—
My Shelter—
My Friend—
My Food for the Journey—
My Journey's End—
You are my breath,
My hope,
My companion,
My craving,
My abundant wealth.
Without You—my Life, my Love—
I would never have wandered across these endless countries.
You have poured out so much grace for me,
Done me so many favors, given me so many gifts—
I look everywhere for Your love—
Then suddenly I am filled with it.
O Captain of my Heart,
Radiant Eye of Yearning in my breast,
I will never be free from You
As long as I live.
Be satisfied with me, Love
And I am satisfied.

O God,
Whenever I listen to the voice of anything You have made—
The rustling of the trees
The trickling of water
The cries of birds
The flickering of shadow
The roar of the wind
The song of the thunder,
I hear it saying:

> God is One!
> Nothing can be compared with God!

Dream Fable

I saw myself in a wide green garden, more beautiful than I could begin to understand. In this garden was a young girl. I said to her, "How wonderful this place is!"

"Would you like to see a place even more wonderful than this?" she asked.

"Oh yes," I answered. Then taking me by the hand, she led me on until we came to a magnificent palace, like nothing that was ever seen by human eyes. The young girl knocked on the door, and someone opened it. Immediately both of us were flooded with light.

God alone knows the inner meaning of the maidens we saw living there. Each one carried in her hand a serving-tray filled with light. The young girl asked the maidens where they were going, and they answered her, "We are looking for someone who was drowned in the sea, and so became a martyr. She never slept at night, not one wink! We are going to rub funeral spices on her body."

"Then rub some on my friend here," the young girl said.

"Once upon a time," said the maidens, "part of this spice and the fragrance of it clung to her body—but then she shied away."

Quickly the young girl let go of my hand, turned, and said to me:

"Your prayers are your light;
Your devotion is your strength;
Sleep is the enemy of both.
Your life is the only opportunity that life can give you.
If you ignore it, if you waste it,
You will only turn into dust."

Then the young girl disappeared.

After an all-night vigil, I prayed to God at dawn, and slept.

In my dream I saw a Tree: green, bright, vast, of indescribable beauty; and on this Tree were three kinds of fruit, such as I had never seen among all the fruits of this world. They shone like the breasts of maidens, red, white, and yellow; they shone like globes and living suns in the green hollows of the Tree. I marveled at them, and asked: "Whose Tree is this?"

A voice replied, "This is your Tree, sprung from the seed of your prayers." Then I began to walk around it, and as I did so I counted eighteen fruits the color of gold, lying on the ground beneath it.

I said, "It would be better if these fruits hadn't fallen, but were still on the Tree."

And the voice answered, "They would be there still except for the fact that while you were praying you kept worrying: 'Did I remember to add the yeast to the dough?' And so they fell, and there they lie."

O God,
Another Night is passing away,
Another Day is rising—
Tell me that I have spent the Night well so I can be at peace,
Or that I have wasted it, so I can mourn for what is lost.
I swear that ever since the first day You brought me back to life,
The day You became my Friend,
I have not slept—
And even if You drive me from your door,
I swear again that we will never be separated—
Because You are alive in my heart.

No-one can repent until God gives him the power.

How long will you keep pounding an open door
Begging for someone to open it?

I don't mourn for the things that *make* me suffer,
But for the things I *fail* to suffer!

I am so afraid of separation
That I have never yet owned a knife.

O God, the stars are shining;
All eyes have closed in sleep:
The kings have locked their doors.
Each lover is alone, in secret, with the one he loves.
And I am here too: alone, hidden from all of them—
With You.

Three Poems in the Spirit of Rabi'a

By Jennifer Doane

The Stones of Men

I have looked for you
in the faces
of all those people
who turn backwards,
like the sun turning towards death,
for fear of you
whom they might see.

I have asked for your whereabouts
everywhere,
and every place upon this earth
has been revealed to me.
I cannot hold
all I see.

Now, if I think about you at all,
I hide it.
I hold my voice back
in the market place
to keep from talking about you.
Today I have not met a single person
who is not heartless;
I have not met a single person
Who does not believe
that I am already staying with you,
whom I am searching for.

These are the stones
given to all men and women.
Not one of us
can live a single day
sitting upon this pile of stones.

The Meeting with God

I, who do not know my own soul's name
have already seen her,
disguised as the shadow of a river,
    saying to me:

"Cry as much as you can
for you cannot live another day
without meeting God.
Your heart cannot be broken more."

When I came back into the world
all those of the world made me forget You
saying I'd loved You more
than anyone could love God;
God would punish me, they all said,
by making me love even more.
How can I pretend not to know You
when I have loved You since
before the day I was born?
You are among a new people,
and my soul has come here
to help me find You.

"Give up the last thing you could own,"
    she says;
"Take the last bite of food out of your
    mouth.
Give up this life."

The Return

You, who I thought
Was so far away—
you, are now standing
in my door.

Look at me—
since you have gone away
I too have become life and death.
The dead child I have put
into the earth,
and the living one I have
hidden away.

The dishes I meant
to set the table with
when you came back
are cracked now,
and I can no longer
buy electricity—

but come, and eat
upon this bright tablecloth,
for toward evening
the sun makes
this whole house glow.

And always, towards evening
I see you
as I saw you five years ago,
about to leave
and about to come back to me
in a single step.
We had just buried the dead child,
and the living child
which you never knew
I am still hiding.

BIBLIOGRAPHY

To those who want to know more about Rabi'a—and Sufi spiritu-
ality in general especially as expressed through its women—I
heartily recommend my sources, in the order in which I discovered
them:

Widad El Sakkani, *First Among Sufis: The Life and Thought of
Rabi'a al-'Adawiyya*, London, Octagon Press, 1982; translated
by Dr. Nabil Safwat.

Dr. Javad Nurbakhsh, *Sufi Women*, New York, Khaniqah
Nimatullahi Publications, 1983; translated by Leonard
Lewisohn.

Margaret Smith, *Rabi'a the Mystic, and Her Fellow Saints in Islam*,
Cambridge University Press, 1928; San Francisco, Rainbow
Bridge, 1977.